FORGOTTEN
BREATHS

I0167207

Poetry

S. Haya

ISBN: 9789914403725

To the hearts my heart
knows, to the wind that blows, and
to the moon that glows.

To those that love me
despite the difficulty,
and those that I love.

Contents

A visit to the bird sanctuary

When our father drove us in,
We were already giggling with anticipation.
We learnt the birds
Were not afraid of people.
The ornithologist told us most of the birds
Had not flown out yet.
We were allowed to feed
The pigeons.
We were so overjoyed that
We jumped over each other.
I remember
Pigeons fighting over grains
On the roof like
It was the stones hitting
Hard. You would think
It was raining.
It was raining
Hard you would think
It was the stones hitting
On the roof. Like
Pigeons fighting over grains.
I remember
We jumped over each other.
We were so overjoyed that
The pigeons
We were allowed to feed
Had not flown out yet.
The ornithologist told us most of the birds
Were not afraid of people.
We learnt the birds.

We were already giggling with anticipation
When our father drove us in.

I killed you

I know you are dead,
As well as all of your kind,
I killed you myself.

What is it you now
Want at my door? Standing here,
Pleading, hat in hand,

With kind rabbit eyes.
You must be out of your mind
Thinking that I would

Not recognize you.
You thought I went blind? You have
Guts my dearest friend.

I must admit, I'm
Shocked. Even in my wildest
Dreams I have never

Imagined this day
Coming. Now I have to do
What one has to do.

Painting the Church

We went to the Old Church and painted it new
yesterday,
Since the deadline for painting all buildings
was due yesterday.

We collected all the remnant paint we could
find
Left on the streets and gave the church a new
hue yesterday.

We woke up each other very early in the
morning
And walked to the church in the morning dew
yesterday.

We took turns using the three brushes we had
Because painting brushes were few yesterday.

We found a hornbill nest with it's babies in the
rafters
Of the apse roof and away they flew yesterday.

We found a thick book on the altar with the
names
Of the saints, most of whom we just knew
yesterday.

The bourgeois that take pride in the newness
Of buildings could not find anyone to sue
yesterday.

4

At midday we were so tired we lay outside
On the grass and watched the sky that was blue
yesterday.

After we've rested today, we'll go back
tomorrow with
Water to water the mango trees we grew
yesterday.

There's my name, Haya, in the corner of the left
nave wall,
Very small, almost illegible, that I drew
yesterday.

The Dinner Guest

The devil is coming for dinner,
He's always punctual and never fails,
He doesn't carry a gift for his sinner.

Don't bother to shave them or to be keener,
Just throw them in with their tails,
The devil is coming for dinner.

When he comes try to be meaner,
"We didn't get time to read the mails,"
He doesn't carry a gift for his sinner.

I wonder whether he's grown fatter or leaner,
I know he still has those long dirty nails,
The devil is coming for dinner.

But tonight, I must become the winner
And show him am done with his frails.
Why doesn't he carry a gift for his sinner?

When he's gone, we'll make the house cleaner
And wash off all his dirty trails.
The devil is coming for dinner
And he'll not be carrying a gift for his sinner.

Silence in the car

Sunday afternoon finds them driving back,
Windows rolled down. Silence.
Radio hissing in lost signal.
The land on both sides lays bare,
A few acacia trees don the landscape
That extends miserably as far as the eye can
see.
The road cuts through like
A drawn line of charcoal on a wall.
Way ahead on the tarmac, a mirage
Floats, an occasional on- coming car
Dances before it comes into focus.
Silence. Radio still hissing.
A few monkeys by the road side
Scramble over an empty cup of yogurt
Someone threw out of a vehicle.
No interest. Silence. Radio hissing.
'Would you rather be a a cow or a donkey?'
Oh Lord! Again. He knows it'll go on and on
About anything and everything.
'A donkey. Because a cow is slaughtered.'
Long silence. Radio still hissing.
He knows it's not over. It cannot be over.
'Would you rather live inside a frog
Or be the frog itself?'
'Inside, at least the sun won't burn me.'
Silence. It's not over.
The radio mumbles. Trees, vegetations
And buildings are coming up. Still no interest.
'Would you rather eat....' 'Look! We are almost,
We are now approaching town, look!'
Silence. No interest. Radio singing *taarab*.

'Would you ra....' 'We will be home soon,
Maybe we should buy milk and bread
Along the way. Want some yogurt?'
'Would you.....'

In my Daughter's Eyes

In my daughter's eyes,
I see the sun rise in the East,
Spreading its polite rays behind the counter,
A radiant yellow sacrament behind the altar.

In my daughter's eyes,
I see lapis lazuri sea waves
Lapping on the rocky shore
Endlessly, until the universe closes its door.

In my daughter's eyes,
I see birds in the azure blue sky,
Gliding smoothly on their spread wings,
No boundaries, no obstacles, no tethers, no strings.

In my daughter's eyes,
I see a young reed in the calm clean river,
Trembling slightly in the flowing waters,
To it, air and light is all that matters.

Lost in a moment

Moments after the
Heavy rain, I am sitting
On the *veranda*

Alone, staring at
Nothing in particular,
Not knowing what to

Think of. My mind is
Asleep while the body is
Still awake and warm.

The cat is testing
Using its delicate paw
For water in the

Mud before it steps.
The rain found it under the
Granary waiting

For a rodent and
Now it has to endure the
The horror of wetting

It's paws. There are small
Ripples in the puddles in
The garden from the

Remnant drizzling drops.
A few short poles stand in the
Garden, decaying

Sisal ropes hanging
Between them, perhaps they were
Props for tomatoes

Or passion fruits, or
Climbing beans, I can't tell, l
Have been away for

Many months. Somebody
Had tried farming, or children
Had tried to high jump.

A sudden hissing
Of potatoes or onion
Put in boiling oil

Jolts me. It's coming
From the kitchen inside the
House behind me.

The rain came and went
And yet I have not even
Moved a finger.

The art of laughing

The art of a good laugh is only well known
To the few people who can partake,
You either learn it or it's inborn.
This esotericism has left many with a fake
Mumble that sounds like a splash in a lake.
A good laugh is as deliberate as the sun,
Not something you do just for its sake.
The art of laughing is not difficult to learn.

A laugh has a life of its own
And trying to kill it is a mistake.
By the time it wants out, it has outgrown
Your body and it should not be put on brake.
A laugh that is not let out will take
A form of an explosion and none
Of your organs will be spared in its wake.
The art of laughing is not difficult to learn.

You need to have your head thrown
Backwards, mouth wide open, for it to make
It's way out to the world. Once it's gone,
Heave out the remnants by trembling shoulders
and neck.
Ribs too - don't stop even if they ache,
Until it's all out. Alternatively, bend forward as
much as you can,
Hands cradling your ribs, and let it all out
without a break.
The art of laughing is not difficult to learn.

A good laugh is a pastry that takes time to
bake,
Not left in the oven too long to burn,
And sits among other pastries as does a cake.
The art of laughing is not difficult to learn.

The Tide is high

The door only got opened
Because my persistent knocking
Would have awakened the children,
The tide is high.

The food was just pushed my way,
Not placed - as is the norm,
And off she went with a pout on her lips,
The tide is high.

A whole yard was left for me on the bed
As she faced the wall
And ignored all my efforts for a chat,
The tide is high.

Maybe it is the whiff in my breath,
Or the time, or a forgotten promise,
God knows what it is this time.
The tide is high.

The Bride and the Broom

There was a new bride,
Who got her mother-in-law's broom
And swept her own house with it.

And the news spread like wild fire,
Like a wave in the sea.

Before panting children
Could struggle out the words,
Their mothers already knew.

It reached the beggars
At the steps of the shops
And they giggled.

It reached the priest
And he squeezed his eyes in thought,
Then made a sign of the cross.

The playing boys heard about it
And threw their heads backwards
In laughter.

The men were caught between
Laughter and sadness,
And they just stared at each other.

The women left their boiling pots,
Adjusted their *kangas* around their waists
And hurried to tell a neighbour,
Who was already containing a laugh.

'The new bride swept her house
With her mother-in-law's broom',
- the young girls whispered and giggled.

The story will be told for years to come,
Boys and girls will tell their grandchildren
Who will also grow to tell the story.

And like all other retold stories,
It will take root in people's minds.
It will only have good and bad things
And no in-betweens anywhere.

Dogs in the Moonlight

They howl their practiced hymn,
Letting it float across the houses,
Stuffing the voids of the silent night,
Indifferent to the emotions it arouses.

A young woman stands at the window,
Leaning on the sadness of her heart,
Praying that today he'll stagger in before
daybreak,
She'll again have to wash off his natural dirt.

A small boy keeps turning on his mat,
His empty stomach won't let him sleep,
Too young to be living one day at a time,
But situations have made it sink in him deep.

A young girl sobs in her bedroom,
Her beddings soak with her innocence,
Her father just left through the door
Back to her snoring mother in silence.

The Act of Coming home

The act of coming home is coming back
To being yourself, or daughter, mother, son
And father, not the badge you were at work.
The act of coming home is quick to learn.
A lot of people sadly get it wrong;
You need to come undressed - leaving badge
And rank at work. You need to learn a song
To hum along the way, and lastly, urge.
(Forgot), another thing you need, is that.
A thing. You need to carry something; food,
A flower, shoes, a shirt, a broken heart,
A smile - a something, warmth, to build the
mood.
Although sometimes a home is not a place,
A home can be a face or mental space.

Dawn will not find me here

It will happen tomorrow and I am very afraid,
At dawn I'll get circumcised and leave my
childhood behind,
My dowry to my father has already been paid.

I eavesdropped at them at the window and felt
betrayed,
My mother and women planning without
sympathy of any kind.
It will happen tomorrow and I am very afraid.

I'll be damned if I ran, I'll be damned if I
stayed,
There's no shelter or safe arms that comes to
my mind,
My dowry to my father has already been paid.

I am meant to be married soon after, I prayed
All prayers and I've no strength left to rewind.
It will happen tomorrow and I am very afraid.

My husband who I've never met before is said
To have three other wives, old and one eye
blind.
My dowry to my father has already been paid.

Dawn will not find me here, the stars will aid
Me see the path to the furthest village I can
find.
It will not happen tomorrow and I am not
afraid,

Even though my dowry to my father has already been paid.

The Cupola

Forgotten,
Standing out like an idiot,
Tall and slender.
Four windows at the top
Facing all the four directions.
Aged walls,
A bats' haven.
A bell hanging in there,
A bell no one uses,
It's uvula hanging in the hollow cup
Like a lone testicle.
A rope hanging in the neck
With a knot at the tip
Where a door opening is.
The priest forgot about it,
The village forgot it's sound.
The steel masts took over
With their beeping lights at night.
We have cellphones now,
With built-in alarms,
What do we do with it now?

A boy with a swamp in his head

I talked with a boy with a swamp
In his head that no one knows
About. I hadn't noticed anything damp
Until we started talking and got close.
He told me that a reed grows
In the middle where the water is deep,
Swamp rats have started to eat his toes,
And at night frogs won't let him sleep.

I found him seated on a tree stump,
Eyes cast in a stare at rows
Of hills in the horizon, palms clump
Together between his knees, eyebrows
Twisted in thought about wars
Raging inside him. He liked to keep
By himself or behind closed doors,
Though at night, frogs didn't let him sleep.

He told me how, once, he tried to jump
Out of himself, about his struggle, his lows,
About how his family continues to dump
More water every day that goes.
He told me how a swamp draws
A laughter from one and soaks it into a weep.
Then I told him about a river that flows,
Because I knew frogs won't let him sleep.

If there's one thing on Earth that restores,
It is time. And talk, talk is not cheap.
In life you can follow all laws
And still frogs won't let you sleep.

The Martyress

The path few can take
You followed your heart along
To make it your own.

Woman, girl, stood by,
We carried you shoulder high
To where heroines lay.

Reed with a stiff spine,
You picked your place yourself
And routed the crowd.

The unspeakable
You spoke, you spoke for many who
Died before they die.

Though the laurel wilts
The name remains forever,
And sown seeds will sprout.

Bad Bones

(a response to Maggie Smith)

Life is long, very long, and the world
Needs to know and make peace with it.
Life is long enough to dream an estimate
Of a million dreams and wake up to a perfect
Sunrise each time. It's a long wait
That should not be spend at one place.

And the world is a beautiful place,
Let no one lie to you. The world
Is such a beautiful place I can't wait
To tell my children about it.
The world is at least 50 percent perfect,
And that's a very conservative estimate.

Life is too long to even bother to estimate
The years one could live. As if to place
A time duration on a life is a perfect
Way of valuing it's worth in the world.
Life is too long that half of it
Has to be spent in sleep as we wait.

People are wonderful and I can't wait
To tell my children about it. An estimate
Of half of the people are good. Isn't it
Awesome? The way it is, there's no place
I would rather be than in the world
Right now. It's interesting and perfect.

Life is long and I've lengthened mine in
perfect,
Deliciously well thought out ways I can't wait
To tell my children and the world.
A thousand perfect ways that in my estimate
Are enough to pass along at any place
I go to as little cotton balls with love in it.

Every difficult has a way through it.
Every dark night is followed by a perfect
Sunrise in the morning that takes it's place.
The morning is for those who wait.
That, to me, seems like a balanced estimate
Of things that I'll tell my children about the
world.

A good estimate, I think a half, of the world
Is perfect. That is the way I see it.
A wonderful place lies out here in wait.

Smoke going back

I am seated at a window
Looking out at a gloomy
Evening after a downpour.
Looking at trees with their
Leaves soaked and still dripping.
Then I see smoke rise
From a chimney beyond the trees
Into the windless sky
Like it had a life of it's own.
Majestic, gaudy and slow
- showing off even.
Rising up like it's carrying secrets,
Something that it knows and we don't.
Secrets of the forest,
Secrets of the lumbermen,
Secrets of the living room,
Secrets of the kitchen.
Carrying them away to heaven,
Like a spy returning home
After years away on duty,
Years of hiding deep under cover,
In planks, timber, branches and stems.
Then going back to tell on us,
So that we find the charge sheet
Already prepared
When we arrive at the pearly gates.

An Ode to baby turtles

Oh! Poor baby turtles
Born into a world of abandonment.
In the sandy beach their mothers lay
Eggs and swim away forever,
Not caring whether they hatch or die.
The eggs only hatch
If they are not unburied and eaten
By seagulls, ghost crabs and other scavengers,
Or smashed by human feet
Jogging, walking, waltzing on the beach.
No single mother turtle knows
Where her children are,
They learn how to survive on their own.
They have to break their egg shells,
Burrow through the sand to the surface,
Then wobble to the water
Where more danger awaits.
They could die from strong currents,
Get entangled in fishermen's nets,
Get chopped in half by motor boat propellers,
Or die from pollution like oil spills and plastic
bags,
Or die from cancer that eats their eyes.
Such an impossible life.

Darkness

I love darkness.
I love it's calmness,
It's engulfing embrace.
I love the privacy it creates,
It's imposing sense of solitude.
How it cuts off the world and turns
The sight inwards. How it lets the heart exhale.
I believe in it's healing power,
How it lets emotions that must be let
To run their course in the body and mind
To have their turn until they burn out.
Emotions that must be let to run
And burn out if you have to heal.
It lets grief run it's course,
And regrets, and anxieties, and heartbreaks.
Rivers have been cried in darkness,
Healing has been found in darkness,
Resolve has been made in darkness,
Happiness has been found in darkness.
I used to be afraid of darkness,
Now I have real fears,
Now I love darkness.
I have fears I must face alone.
Only darkness makes me be alone.

There was no darkness

My grandmother told me a story about
How as little girls
They'd run away and hide for days
With their mothers and father's
In the reeds
When colonialists came
To their village with sugar.
How they forced them to take it,
How they whipped those who didn't.
They didn't need it,
They didn't want it,
They loved their millet porridge
Just the way it was.
Good taste is a perception.
Their religious beliefs were
Condemned and labelled as primitive.
Father Whittenberg - who they called Obago,
Told them that his God was better,
As if there was a world ranking of Gods.
They had names,
Good names,
Names that had meaning
To them - ancestry, seasons, character, weather,
But Father Obago told them
That those names were shady,
That they needed proper names,
Good names,
English names.
He also insisted that his traditional
Form of dressing was better than theirs.
And so men had to wear suits
And a necktie,

He said it was official.
And brides had to wear a white gown
On their wedding day.

Joys of movement

Depending on the
Season, birds migrate from one
Place to another.

Without a border,
The whole world is their house,
They sit on anything.

They are sustained
By freedom, movement is a
Part of their living.

How unfair would it
Be to put nets in the sky
To restrict their flight.

What is life if you
Have everything but cannot
Move anywhere?

And humans are just
Like birds - creatures of movement.
This is our house.

Lost in the Hills

The woman who found me said I'll not kneel
properly
Until I let the wound on the knee heal properly.

She had carried me to her house with ease
Although I had not submitted to her will
properly.

She put a pot on wood fire and started filling it
With water, she stopped before it could fill
properly.

She then cleaned out the wound with trained
hands
Of someone who had mastered the skill
properly.

She applied a paste with a foul smell from
A bottle with a lid that she later had to seal
properly.

She brought me a cup of soup she'd cooked
From herbs whose identity she did not reveal
properly.

Looks like I'll have to end my excursion and try
again
Next year, since I cannot climb the hill
properly.

I told her my name is Haya and she chuckled with
Satisfaction, like someone who has sealed a deal properly.

Fences

Peak of the hill we are standing and
Looking at thatches that roof all our
Future and present, the past is not
Worthy of thinking about. In a
Moment like these, all our life is a
Picture across the expansive and
Peaceable village. The sun is now
Setting behind, on our backs as we
Look at the huts in a silence that
Feeds on our thoughts and the memories.
Joining the huts we can see the small
Paths that have formed from seasons of
Walking between them like channels that
Feed all the separate cells of the
Body. As we watch it we realize
Fences are missing, absent from the
Picture. Perhaps, that is why it is
Looking superb, like a scene from the
Movies. You tap at my shoulder to
Indicate night is approaching. We
Need to begin the descent to the
Village, the darkness is closing in.

Thunderstorm

It starts with flashes
Of lightening blinking
In my brain,
And I become psychic.
It rains in my heart,
A torrent that soaks
And carry every debris.
It gets muddy and soggy
Like a freshly ploughed
Arrow root field
Because the soil
Is always loose.
And the wind blows
From my flared nostrils,
Scattering papers on the desk
And carrying a poem to the sea,
Sometimes breaking tree branches
And carrying roofs away.
And when thunder strikes,
I've to cough it out.

Love is a poem

Love is a poem,
Measured, unmeasured.
Innocent,
Sitting on a page
Like a pigeon,
Ensnaring,
Not pleading.
Thirsty,
If you fall for it,
That is it.
You can't resist it.

Short or long,
A haiku sometimes,
A villanelle maybe,
With repetitions along.
Or a sonnet
With spelt boundaries.
Or free,
So many forms.

Words choosing where to sit
By themselves,
You only need to arrange
The seats.

A lover showing up
The moment you create space
In your heart, for them.

A line, and a spark
Lights up a dry country.
A country you had no idea
It existed.
A country in your heart.

You hear murmurs of flames
And splinters of burning wood
In your dreams.

A fire starts inside your body,
The world is different,
And happiness is your mother.

Saudade

I cannot believe I'll never hold you again,
You slipped through my fingers into air,
The memories you left are a source of pain.

Your hearty laughter still rings in my brain,
- i can even draw it. Yours was a laughter so
rare.
I cannot believe I'll never hear you again.

On everything you touched you left a grain
Of yourself, your kindness and care.
The memories you left are a source of pain.

I run my fingers through the scarf edge and
refrain
From thinking, cafuné, the texture of your hair,
I cannot believe I'll never touch you again.

We ate in the shade, sung in the sun and danced
in the rain,
You socked me with your love without spare,
The memories you left are a source of pain.

The plans we wrote for ourself are now vain
Because when you left, you left despair.
I cannot believe I'll never see you again,
The memories you left are a source of pain.

A name

I can make a case, in fact I do, often,
That the ability to write a name will
Always remain with oneself and cannot be
taken
Away from them. Unless the aim is to kill
What they really are, you should never feel
That you can do it. The name will not be the
same.
They can be siblings, or parents, or friends, but
still
No one can write another human's name.

It's one who determines if their name is
forgotten
Or remains glued in people's minds with a seal
Of infinity, way after their generation has
fallen.
Once a name is written, it stands out like a hill,
It cannot be hidden, or be shared like a bill.
It's one themselves who build their fame
Or make themselves anonymous, because for
real,
No one can write another human's name.

I've seen those whose names have been eaten
By goats that roam streets looking for a meal.
Some have left theirs unattended and stolen
By thieves looking for something to steal.
Yet, a name is what you find when you peal
Everything else away and remain with a frame,
And it's built by a deed, - a good or an ill.
No one can write another human's name.

So, once you build yours, treat it with a great
deal
Of care. Keep it safe or you will blame
Yourself when the work you put in sums to nil.
No one can write another human's name.

Secrets

The secret to happiness start
With doing what pleases your heart.
The moment you let
Your life to be set
By people, you stand to be hurt.

The secret to happiness lies
In knowing exactly the price
Of time that you waste
On worrying how best
To please the whole world and its eyes.

The secret to happiness rest
In leaving the things you detest,
And people that dim
The lights in your dream.
They stand in the way of your best.

The secret to happiness lives
In eating and drinking what gives
Your cells what they need.
Not toxins that breed
A monster that never forgives.

The secret to happiness grows
From reading a book, for it blows
Your thinking away.
A book that can stay
With you, when you shop at the stores.

Other secrets just for fun

The secret to peace of your mind
Is searching your inner to find
Contentment in life,
Accepting that strife
Is part of a low of a kind.

The secret to laughter is found
In letting it start like a sound
A chicken would make,
Allow it to take
You captive and shake you around.

The secret to sleeping in peace
Is working with passion of bees
On things that you love
And flying above
The clouds, in the neck of the breeze.

The secret to confidence rest
In knowing your strength for the test
Ahead, and to find
That strength in your mind,
Then put it in use for the best.

Dreaming

Calm down,
It was just a dream.
Here, wipe your brow,
I am here with you,
It was just a dream.
Relax.
That is the way it is,
One doesn't get to hit the ground,
You come falling down and wailing,
Kicking in the air,
Nothing to grasp on,
Struggling to catch a breath.
Just when you are about to hit the ground,
You wake up.
You wake up
Just when you are about to hit the ground.
Struggling to catch a breath,
Nothing to grasp on,
Kicking in the air,
You come falling down and wailing.
One doesn't get to hit the ground,
That is the way it is.
Relax,
It was just a dream,
I am here with you.
Here, wipe your brow,
It was just a dream,
Calm down.

The journey on a Bus

I
The engine humming at high gear,
Children asleep in their mothers' laps
While adults are struggling to stay
Awake, some lost in thought.
The radio mumbling something.
Small sacs with arrow roots
Or potatoes and chicken in cartons
With holed sides under some seats.
I sit by the window looking out.

II
The tea plantations
Laid out on hillsides and valleys
Like slabs laid out by God,
Or expansive mattresses,
Beaming in greenness.
The paths cut through it
In squares and rectangles
Like they were measured by a ruler.

III
Hawkers at the windows
When the bus pulls over.
Selling water, juice, *khat*,
Pliers, socks, roast maize
On cob smeared with a lemon
Cut in half and dipped in pepper powder,
Boiled eggs with *kachumbari.*
Babies wailing,
People alighting to relieve themselves.

IV
The evening sun on my side,
Radio airing the evening drive.
People awake with anticipation.
We are almost there.

The flu

the houses now
have people during the day,
windows are open.

families now eat
together as should be norm
all meals of the day.

spouses are knowing
each other after years
of married rat race.

the children are home
because their schools are closed
indefinitely.

pets are delighted
of friendship they are getting
the entire week.

the kitchen table
turned into an office
desk with a laptop.

board meetings are held
online, in pressed shirts, ties,
shorts, bathroom sandals.

the world is breathing

after a long period of
smoke suffocation.

kilimanjaro
can now be seen from rooftops
of nairobi.

it seems that the flu
is what the world needed to
heal itself from rot.

the world is telling
us that it can just do fine
without us, humans.

A stroll at night in the city

As I take a stroll at night in the city,
I pass a man selling mint sweets and biscuits
Spread out on a makeshift carton stand.
Three street boys are playing a game of cards
Under the glow of a street lamp.
A face under a hat is lighting a cigarette
Leaning on a lamp post and in a trench coat.
A family is sleeping under a footbridge.
I hear music from a nearby club as
Whores in skimpy cloths stand in small groups
Along the street, territorially spread out.
A woman is selling *chapatis* and coffee
To those sitting on a bench she has put out,
Some hunched over their phones like praying
apostles.
The city and its people do not sleep.
The city and its people do not sleep,
Some hunched over their phones like praying
apostles.
To those sitting on a bench she has put out,
A woman is selling *chapatis* and coffee.
Along the street, territorially spread out,
Whores in skimpy cloths stand in small groups.
I hear music from a nearby club as
A family is sleeping under a footbridge.
Leaning on a lamp post and in a trench coat
A face under a hat is lighting a cigarette
Under the glow of a street lamp.
Three street boys are playing a game of cards
Spread out on a makeshift carton stand.
I pass a man selling mint sweets and biscuits
As I take a stroll at night in the city.

The new normal

There was a time we moved everywhere
without rigidity,
Without roadblocks by doctors after every
other bend,
Now we are locked up and stuck in this city.

We used to whinge all day about frivolity,
Now we have to watch how we spend.
Gone are days of shopping without rigidity.

The flu has written new rules of commit,
We cannot travel to the village over the
weekend
To see our grandparents, we are stuck in this
city.

Humanity is struggling to fight the natural
proclivity
For hugs and handshakes. A new milieu we
can't comprehend.
We miss the socialization that had no rigidity.

The eyes that smiled and mouths that were
witty
Are now forlorn, though mostly they pretend.
It's all because we are stuck in this city.

My heart weeps for the annihilated sense of community.
That, I feel, is one thing we must all defend.
There was a time we moved everywhere without rigidity,
Now we are locked up and stuck in this city.

.

Days and Nights

The days are for laughing aloud
And wearing a face in the crowd.
A face that is fake,
As fake as a flake.
A show that I cast that is fraud.

The days are for smiling from ear
To ear like a flower the year
Has favored. The smile
Is just for a while
Until it's replaced by fear.

The days are for chatting around
The office and stomping the ground
In dances to fill
The hollowness till
A high that is faulty is found.

The nights are for weeping in sobs.
The foam in the pillow absorbs
The tears from the eyes.
The spirit that lies
In dark is adjusting its robes.

The nights are for fighting the ghosts
That howl in my head. These are costs
Of living a lie,
Of wanting to die,
Denial and opting for toasts.

The nights are for trembling in fear

And sweating, for anger that's clear
As salt, for a dose
Of truth, for a force
In blood, and the thirst for a beer.

Grief

No other person can feel
How you feel in grief.
How can they
When they are not you?
How can they
When you lost different things?
You can grieve the same person
But you lost different things.
Grief is personal, like a fingerprint,
A sensation that cannot be shared.
Nobody can grieve on your behalf,
It demands your personal attention,
It's a fever that has to be sat through.
When it hits you,
There's no telling how long it'll stay.
Allow yourself to nurse it inside
And decimate it slowly.

A Sestina

I can't believe
Am still in love with the idea
Of love and that I actually think
There's still someone out there
For me. I find it laughable that
I still don't find it dull.

Of course, I mean dull
In a good way, there are people who still
believe
In love out there, and I respect that.
What I find funny with such an idea
In my mind is that it could still be there.
I can possibly think

Of many reasons it shouldn't, but I can't think
Of any reason it should. It should be dull
To me by now, considering that there
Have been numerous heartbreaks that I believe
Were completely unnecessary. An idea
Shouldn't be such stubborn that

No amount of heartbreak can bleach it. That
Is sad and feels like addiction when you think
About it, like slavery, like a yoke of an idea
Around your neck. If it's not dull
To me by now, then I don't believe
That even in future there

Will be a way out, unless there
Is another unknown closure to that.
Here is what I believe
Though, and when I think
About it, although it seemed like a dull
Idea in the first place, it's a good idea.

I believe the whole notion and idea
Of love is just conjecture, there
Is nothing to it. It may seem like a dull
Thing to say, but it is just that.
Like life after death, we sometimes think
It doesn't exist, but mostly, we believe

It does. And that doesn't mean that there
Are people that believe in another idea.
For me, I think I now want it to be dull.

Death

Death is a biological occurrence
Only to the dead ones.
To the living,
It's a state of mind.
For I know a man who died
The day we met and talked,
And when I left,
I knew he was dead.
We met again after two years
And that is when I buried him.
A man I had wanted to meet for years.
So, when I received a call
That he was dead, I felt nothing.
I had already gone through that.
We choose whether the dead
Continue living with us
Or the living get dead and forgotten.

Leaving

Leave when you feel like leaving,
Even when nobody has ever left,
Just leave,
You are not nobody.
If you ever miss where you have left,
Don't feel bad about it,
It is ok to miss.
There is a reason
Why you felt like leaving.
Leaving is a natural animal response.
Leaving is a process,
Your mind can precede you
Or you can leave it behind.

Me and Myself

When I leave, I'll carry
Myself with me
Like a nomad
Who has exhausted
What the present can offer.
I will not look back.
I will not miss back.
I will not think back.
Not like last time
When I left
And had to come back
For myself.
We don't leave each other
These days,
We have learned
To live within each other.

Insomnia

There are times I wake
Up to listen to
The night, or the night
Wakes me up to talk
To me, I don't know.
An intimate time
Just between the two
Of us. The moments
Of truth, of fear,
Of anxiety,
Of despondence, of
Depression and stress,
Of panic attacks.
The moment to think
About my life in
The silence of the
Sleeping world. They are
Sad and desperate
Moments of pining.
Why sleep abandons
Me when I need it
Most I do not know.

Freedom

I am free now,
Now that nobody loves me.
I am free from the obligation
Of reciprocity.
I am in the bliss of indifference.
It's wonderful here,
A spectacular province,
The scenery is perfect
And the mind is clear.
Nothing needs to be remembered.
Give me anything but love,
Love is too heavy,
I can't bear it.

Self love

love yourself when you are lost
love yourself when you don't know
what you are
love yourself in pain
love yourself in despondency
love yourself in sequestration
love yourself in rejection
love yourself when the road hits a dead end
love yourself the morning after
love yourself when you are not worth any love
love yourself when you are at the bottom of the
barrel
it's the only thing you deserve
it's the only thing you owe yourself
it's the last thread holding you from falling into
the abyss
once it breaks no one else can help you
nourish that single thread and make it strong
it's the only dependable love thread

Depression

Down my heart a pit is extending every
Night and day without indication bottom
Rock will come. Sometimes it is good to hit the
Bottom than keep on

Sinking, grasping, kicking without a landing.
Bottom gives you stability, start, a sight than
Days of sinking. Sinking exhausts you,
  drains your
Hope to recover.

Darkness fills all spaces where hope and
purpose
Lived before the fall. In the darkness ghosts of
Sadness look at me in the eyes and see their
Own in denial.

Days are full of days of their own and
  nights are
Walks through arid lands of the world
  without a
Drop of water. Dates are forgotten - lost in
Spells of apathy.

Body cannot do things that I loved doing,
Things have lost their taste. I am trying
  hard to
Nurse severe disinterest but a bit of
Poetry writing.

Day by day I live in a shadow cast by
Pride, deceit and ego. I need assistance,

Yet, refuse to ask or to show I need the
Help in my sadness.

Maybe, maybe writing this sapphic gives the
Landing needed. Finding a rock, a stepping
Stone to place your foot on is what I needed
Hopelessly, badly.

The season

It was the year of circumcision,
The village was covered with
A permanent jubilatory air.
Two years of waiting
Had bottled enough anticipation.
Boys had long grouped themselves,
Based on friendship,
As units that will face the knife together.
A brotherhood that will
Remain until death.
Uncles had separated chicken
To be given out as gifts
And fathers were ready with
Goats for the festivities.
And then the season had arrived,
Everyone lined the roads
To cheer the initiates
Splashed with white ash paint
As they rung the jingle
And sung the season's songs.
On the morning of the big day
The initiates were taken
To the river at dawn and immersed
In the water to wash off their
Childhood, and smeared with mud.
They then walked back to face
The knife; standing astride
And looking up to the sky
Without blinking an eye
Amidst jubilation from the crowd.

The most beautiful woman

It was the beauty in the woman
It lay in her acceptance of the
    banality of her face
It lay in her unapologeticness
    about her unsightliness
It lay in her confidence in being
It lay in the fullness of her confidence
It lay in the unpretentiousness of
    her laughter
It lay in the genuineness of her
    happiness
It lay in the infectiousness of her
    smile
It lay in her unshakeable resolve not
    to seek anybody's validation
It lay in her fidelity in following her
    heart
It lay in her jealousness in ownership
    of her happiness
It was breathtaking beauty
It was beauty that will never not impress

Champions

I see them out for the morning run,
Slender like impalas,
Strength oozing out of their toned long legs.
In groups and some solitary,
Cutting through the morning air with ease,
Soles not touching the ground long enough.
Tea pickers and school children waving in
admiration.
Conquerors of marathons of the world,
The world lays out medals in cities for them to
collect.
42 is nothing, time is the competition,
Under 2 hours is the new challenge.

The alarm bird

Always on time and
Without missing a day, the
Bird let's out a tune.

The bird of the sun,
Waits the sun to be Midway
To give an alarm.

Not easy to spot,
Camouflaged in the trees
From where it sings.

Mothers know it's time
To put lunch pots on fire
And set the table.

Herders know it's time
To take cattle for water
Down the river.

The Nairobian

There has to be a line
About a Nairobi woman who has made it.
Sunday morning, she is driving
To church from her leafy suburb,
Not just any church, a classy church.
The route will have her pass by a slum
And she has the windows rolled up
To wade off miserable begging hands of slum
kids.
That slum has girls who cannot afford sanitary
pads,
Abandoned children who have not eaten for
days,
And mothers with sick children
Without money to take them to hospitals.
She knows.
In her purse is a stack of crisp notes
For tithe and fundraising at the church,
The pastor has to upgrade to the latest ride.
In the evening she'll take her pet dog
And herself for massage and spa treatment,
Because, you know, you only live once.
There has to be another line
About an underage house maid in her house
That she overworks, mistreats and underpays.
There has to be a line too about her husband
Who she leaves without breakfast because
She's in a hurry to go and pray for her
marriage.

The Savior is born

Behold the world, for He is born,
Climb on the hill and blow the trumpet,
Son of the one who sits on the throne.

The wise men from the East were shown
The way by the star to where it set,
Behold the world, for He is born.

Born of the Virgin from one of our own,
He has come to save the world from its fate,
Son of the one who sits on the throne.

In gold, silver and bronze let us adorn
Him, let us make this day great.
Behold the world, for He is born.

Dance and rejoice, let it be known
The world over how it was told by the prophet,
Son of the one who sits on the throne.

In Bethlehem there's the sound of the horn
And gifts of spices and perfume at the gate,
Behold the world, for He is born,
Son of the one who sits on the throne.

Children of Nairobi River

Floating in the black murk,
Going wherever the river takes them
As it winds through the slums
And through the leafy suburbs.
Some with skin ashen with newness,
Hair still damp with sliminess,
Placenta issuing at the tummy
Like a frontal tail
With networks of tiny blood veins.
Some with streaks of blood
All over their bodies.
Some disfigured,
A head missing, a limp, anything.
Eyes squeezed into two pits of wrinkles,
Small stubby fingers
Frozen in a tight grip,
(A grip at a chance not given,)
To form a small fist,
Or fingers wiggling to grasp at anything.
Some long dead,
Some opening their mouths
To take their first gulp,
A gulp of raw sewage.
In foetal positions, or stiff,
Or limply and flexible.
The children of the river,
She embraces them
Like a mother that she is.
Unwanted anywhere else,
Dumped in every night.
Some wrapped in plastic paper bags
And yacked with a wide arc

To the middle of the river,
And she welcomes them with a splash
Because these are her children.

One day I'll come back to this place

One day I'll come back
To let the tadpoles nibble
At my toes, and to scoop
The jelly-dots-beads-eggs
Of frogs with my palm.
To splash water on glossy leaves
And lazy blades of grass.

One day I'll come back
To wade through a fog
Of solitude lying wasted.
To toss a pebble in the water
And let that amuse me.
To feed the small cerise birds
Whose foremothers drunk at the river.

One day I'll come back
To this place, to point at a tree
I used to sit under, or a stump,
Or 'a tree used to be here.'
To watch the sun as it sets,
(Not the sunset,)
Yellow as a york,
And wish I could go with it.

Of knowing

I
Of their sniggering remarks
Of contempt
Of disdain
Of uselessness
Of cold dislike
Of valuelessness
Of worthlessness
Of cold treatment
Of sequestration
Of humiliation

II
Of his joblessness
Of despondency
Of depression
Of sleepless nights
Of bad chest pains at night
Of muscle spasms
Of year after year after year
Of knowing family won't help
Of lost sense of family
Of thinking life is not worth it
Of lost enthusiasm in life
Of questions

III
Of impromptu family seminars in the kitchen
or on the phone to vilify him.
Of his learning that how people make him feel
is everything, not what they do for him.
Of realizing they'll mourn a death, not him.

IV
Of trying his best
Of keeping quiet
Of knowing he is in it alone
Of resolve
Of remaining dead
Of knowing
Of finding comfort in despair
Of stumbling on a villanelle and a sonnet
Of trying it out
Of page after page
Of a new life
Of leaving the world behind

Of pasts and lessons

What is a sea
Without a shipwreck?
A sea worth its salt
Must have a shipwreck
Buried down its belly,
From years of being.

A past
A fault
A disaster
A testimony

What is a Saint
Without a sin?

What is grey hair
Without a heartbreak?

The devil knows,
More because he is old
Than because he is the devil.

Of days without color

These days, my days have lost their color,
I wake up to stare at another one
Without a thread of enthusiasm in me.
My days taste like they have already
Been lived by someone else
And left behind, tasteless.
I don't get a fresh and new day
Of my own anymore.
My days seem like having to open
The same gift box every day,
The gift box you packed yourself,
For yourself.
My days have lost their mystery.
I try to write a sapphic stanza
And it turns out sad.
I think of an appropriate dactyl
And trochee phrase to end it,
'Stuck at the bottom' will do,
Or maybe 'Starting another',
Or perhaps 'Tired of living'.

Blood

Hot,
The confidence it wilts
Takes ages to sprout again,
Or never.
It scotches happiness,
It burns joy
Back into the ground.

Sticky,
Holding onto itself
Like a dough of wheat flour,
Not easy to pull apart,
Tentacles always pulling back to itself.
A lump of glue,
A lump you always want to be in,
A lump you know you'll always be in,
A lump you wish you can pinch away from,
A lump you want to pinch away from.

Thick,
Thicker in having and having,
Or lacking and lacking.
Thins with having and lacking,
Or lacking and having.

Love me today

Love me today in this fog,
When the sun has hidden
From my face,
When my basket has nothing in.
Love me today when it's difficult,
Love me today when choices
Are spread on your table.
Don't love me when it's easy,
Don't love me because choices are out.
Love me when my skin is ashen
with nothingness.
When I have nothing to give,
When am wanted and needed,
That is when I know.
When at the bottom of the barrel,
That is when I know.
When you don't need to say it,
That is when I know.
You don't need to say,
I'll know,
Saying blinds and numbs sometimes.

A Rustler's song

Tonight, we are going to Samburu to raid,
Only the cowards will remain behind,
We are Pokots, we are never afraid.

Our blood that they spilled has to be paid,
We are going to take any cattle we find,
Tonight, we are going to Samburu to raid.

We'll kill their men and leave virgins laid,
We will burn granaries and houses of any kind,
We are Pokots, we are never afraid.

Girls will not marry the cowards who stayed
Behind, unless they are blind.
Tonight, we are going to Samburu to raid.

The elders have drunk from a gourd and
sprayed
On us the powder they took time to grind.
We are Pokots, we are never afraid.

He with a beard before he goes for a raid is said
To be a child and not right in his mind.
Tonight, we are going to Samburu for a raid,
We are Pokots, we are never afraid.

Jini

I've walked from the sea bottom
To the shore.
Standing on the beach,
The sea behind me.
Two rivulets forming at the heals
Where I stand back to the sea.
A strand of seaweed above
The eye (I'll remove it,)
And probably in the armpit
(I'll check the discomfort.)

These faces,
Most were born just the other day,
They never saw me.
The shock on their faces.
The dropped money and fish
From frozen hands.
The forgotten conversations midway,
The fizzled laughters.
The silence.
The eyes.

My fury is not for them.
It's for her,
In the brick house.
Maybe by the window
- sipping tea,
Or just staring out.
Maybe sleeping in the bed
With a Bible, or a rosary, or a pork bone,
Or whatever she has this time
On the bedside table,

Or under the pillow.
And him
(Most definitely him.)

A pantoum to the pilgrimage of turtles

It's the most gorgeous thing I've seen,
An army of newly hatched baby turtles
Wabbling on the beach to the sea
And motivated by an innate urge to survive.

An army of newly hatched baby turtles
Emerging underground from buried eggs
And motivated by an innate urge to survive
All heading to the water like pilgrims.

Emerging underground from buried eggs
Like magical creatures sprouting from the sand.
All heading to the water like pilgrims,
Undirected, pulled by the smell of the sea.

Like magical creatures sprouting from the sand
The turtles know their way themselves,
Undirected, pulled by the smell of the sea.
I just stood there watching until the sun was
hot.

The turtles know their way themselves,
Wabbling on the beach to the sea,
I just stood there watching until the sun was
hot,
It's the most gorgeous thing I've seen.

Africa

Is it your black allure that chides the world?
Today your sons and daughters bawl on streets
For justice, bullets aim at us like veld
Impalas, cops are called on us in fleets.
So tell me mother, what is it you did
To make the world irascible? Anger flows
On streets, in playing fields, in news we read
And watch in shock, and yet the killing grows.
It's not your fault the world has picked the shade
Of skin you passed to us (as genes) to judge
Our traits. The fault is world's. It sorts instead
Of getting people's cultures mix and merge.
The time to end the bias that's based on race
Is now, right now, we need to live in peace.

A midnight Lament

Oh, Dear my lover
Who belongs to the future,
We should meet very soon.

Oh, Dear my sweetheart
Who dances in my sweet dreams,
I want to touch your hand.

Oh, Dear my soul mate
Who is hiding behind air,
These silly games should stop.

Oh, Dear my best friend
Who acts like I don't exist,
Stop looking past me.

Oh, Dear my partner
Who has never been present,
I want to keep you warm.

They have come, again

They've brought their painted faces,
And their long horse hairs sway,
They've brought their funny gazes.

Now they're going to hold me in phases
And Mo won't take me away,
They've brought their painted faces.

They'll laugh and eat small cakes Mo places
Before them on that nice cream tray,
They've brought their funny gazes.

They'll sit awkwardly in their small dresses,
And while they're here Mo won't look my way.
They've brought their painted faces.

I now know their thoughts without guesses;
"He's so cute," they will all say,
They've brought their funny gazes.

And long after they've gone, lingering traces
Of their flower smell will still stay.
They've brought their painted faces.
They've brought their funny gazes.

The village dancer

She moves like an excited dragon fly,
Awakening fires that quietly lie
In our loins – the kind that excruciates.
She's the twin sister to one of the initiates,
Her proud mother must have passed her some,
It shows in the tremble of her bare bosom.

Whether she has a bone – no one can tell,
All the time smiling - delighted in casting a
spell,
She flies the sisal skirt with her chocolate hips,
Creating a scene in this sunset that keeps
The eyes open in dust. Too shocked to cheer,
We nod to the instrument neither of us can
hear.

She has raised the stakes for her hand,
A battle for a true daughter of our land
Is fast brewing. She moves in those ways
That makes a man's blood boil, one of these
days
She'll have a head brought to her on a platter.
She'd better never dance before the one who
matter.

The beard

A man was fast driving his car,
Enjoying the breeze from the star
And saw a bad sheep,
And thought of a heap
Of rugs with a stench from a far.

He slowed down the car to a halt,
Then scratched his head and then thought,
He looked at the mirror
And felt a little horror,
Then realised it was his own fault.

He ran to the shop and then said;
"I want a sharp blade ever made,
Am done with this earth."
Then took in a breath,
And quick he just cut off his head.

Sunset in the Village

A polite sunset turns the earth's mold
Into a stretched rugged bed of gold.

It makes the serenading pair
Of birds send tunes into windless air.

The sweet smell of nature's bosom
Makes breathing itself awesome.

A line of returning cattle at a distance
Take each step with a lazy sense,

In peculiar order as the bull leads,
Herdsmen behind – like a chain of beads.

Boys pick their shirts from a heap,
After a game their memories will keep.

The rhythmic thumping echo of pestle
Reaching only those who stain a little.

Girls gracefully balancing their pots
From the river, smiling at their thoughts.

It will be a forbidding perfidy to say
There will ever be a stormy or sad day.

Queen of the Night

I am the queen of the night,
Stop trying, you know you can't,
You will never reach my height.

Don't ever think I'll start a fight,
You can still do whatever you want
But I am the queen of the night.

You can sit before the white light
And bask until you get burnt,
But you will never reach my height.

The green monster in your chest bite,
I hear you shift in your chair and grunt,
I am the queen of the night.

You have nothing for the sight
And your eccentricities are blunt,
You will never reach my height.

You do not know how to do it right,
How come you haven't learnt
That I am the queen of the night?
You will never reach my height.

The picture

In my mother's house, there is a picture
On the wall, in a varnished frame,
Of a man with unspoken name,
And a steady gaze of a watcher.

In my mother's house, there is a flame
Without the warmth of presence,
And although life has no fence,
Every day is just the same.

In my mother's house, there is silence
Throughout an interesting conversation,
And although jokes can be in rotation,
They don't erase the absence so intense.

In my mother's house, there is legislation
That nobody recalls having passed,
But which everyone obeys to the last,
About not asking the sacred question.

In my mother's house, I have grown fast
Because circumstances are the best teacher.
What is in the house is just a picture,
I also know this is not the worst.

The Sea

The sky is changing; pets now jump in loops,
A hanging sea now lets a roaring sound,
Converging clouds are pulling close like troops
Of soldiers getting set to pound the ground.
A feeling hangs in air that makes a bird
Just stop its search for grain and find its pair.
The cows in shed have stopped chewing cud,
The men in huts exchange a knowing stare.

The dust on playing ground will go away,
The grass will grow and kids will play all day.
The smell of earth expectant mothers know
Will make a few to pick on wall at door.
The men will walk around the farm while worn
In coats to test how deep the rain has gone.

My neighbour's daughter

Things my neighbour's daughter has done have left the
Quiescent village hissing in gossip whispers
Never heard before, and the sick are also
Bursting in laughter.

Women lean on fences to share the juiciest
Version going around and then backwards toss their
Heads to let the throatiest of laughter out when
Husbands are gone off.

Men are caught confused between a laugh and
Anger, smiling, shaking their heads, not knowing
What to say. They pray their own daughters never
Pull such a drama.

'Stay away and move to a town where answers
Never get recalled if you ever want to
Get a husband loving and deaf enough for
Happiness ending.'

A witch weed

A witch weed has grown in my house
And it's all my fault.
Started as a small crack on the floor,
Right in the middle of the house
Where I cannot conceal with a pot.
Formed a small bump in the earth
Before it showed its shoot.

A witch weed has grown in my house
And it's all my fault.
The fire must not have killed all the seeds
Before I made a circle of holes
For wood posts that hold the roof,
And smeared the floor with cow dung
Mixed with white clay from the riverside.

A witch weed has grown in my house
And it's all my fault.
Now what will I do?
Should I uproot it with its roots
And let one of my children die?
Or should I strike it with my walking stick
And let my own arm swell?

A witch weed has grown in my house
And it's all my fault.
Soon, someone will see its shoot
And tell the whole village
How a witch weed has grown in my house,
And mothers will push their children
Behind their skirts when I pass.

The Evening Chant

Come,
Come closer,
The fire of my heart,
Now tell me,
Who promised to always be here?
Yes,
And who is still here?
Yes,
And I will always be here.

The hair is white,
The sheen is gone,
But tell me,
Who still strokes it?
Yes,
And I will still stroke it.

The fingers are knobbed,
But tell me,
Who still holds them?
Yes,
And I will still hold them.

The skin is crumpled
And grown scaly,
Who still caresses it?
Yes,
And I will still caress it.

I made a promise to you
Long time ago,
Remember?

No?
But I'll still keep it,
Even when you don't remember it.

I will hold on

Let the fog engulf all the trees along the
Path that leads to mountains of flowing
Milk and honey, let it impair my sight and
Block my near future.

Let the darkness press on my opened eyes and
Sneak to fill any space it had overlooked,
Let it fill my nose and soak my lungs with
Fear of the darkness.

Let the raining clouds of the season come and
Hang above my house and then pour all season,
Let the flooding pour through the door and get
my
Happiness drenched.

Nights are always followed by days of
brightness,
Fruits will rot and smell, but the seeds will
sprout and
Grow to trees that feed all. The fruits of
patience
Drop in the morning.

The Nest

Every bird knows how to make her nest,
To lay her eggs away from bad eyes,
Every bird struggle and does her best.

Working to finish before the sun goes west
It starts to build the nest before sunrise,
Every bird knows how to build her nest.

Working the whole day without a rest,
Putting in a lot of commitment and sacrifice,
Every bird struggle and does her best.

It can either use dust, made into a paste,
Or it can use sticks, or even straws of rice,
Every bird knows how to make her nest.

It can either build under a bridge or on a crest,
Or deep in the forest where the ghost lies,
Every bird struggle and does her best.

The struggle (maybe) will make her eggs
blessed
To hatch and then grow to rule the skies,
Every bird knows how to make her nest,
Every bird struggle and does her best.

The Walk back home

Returning back from field as norm,
Along a path that takes them home,
They walk to form a line of humps
And horns that move in swings and jumps.

Their bellies bulging out like sacks
Of millet after harvesting works,
Their hooves are trumping earth to raise
Some dust and drum a song of praise.

The biggest bull is leading pack
In front as calves trail at back,
A pecking order set without
A bruising fight to win or shout.

The herder taking steps behind,
He has no thought to cark his mind.
His hands are stretched out and rests
On stick along his shoulders at wrists.

The sun awaits a moment's sign
Before it sinks behind the line,
It washes fields in glowing gold
And makes shadows stand out bold.

How like a play is a day

I
A day unfolds it's self like a play
On stage. The curtains open in the morning
And the stage is lit throughout the day
Until the curtains close again in the evening.

The cast goes through their cues
From scripts unknown to them unrehearsed.
Nothing is random, nothing is news,
Everything is arranged and cannot be reversed.

A bread delivery man is setting up crates
In front of the shop. He counts and writes
Down on a paper as the shopkeeper takes
Them inside. His engine is left running and the
lights

Are still on, - he's in a hurry to get
To the next shop before it's too late.

II
To the next shop before it's too late
A girl is going to buy a morning after pill
After a night with a man she met
At the bar. The events of last night still

Hazy in her mind before they are replaced
By events of the new day. She lives
Her life a day at a time, yesterday is phased
Out by today and whatever that life gives.

The shoe shiner is setting up his stall
Along the street, his brushes and shoe polish
tins
Ready. A wet rag too, should the customer's
sole
Need to be wiped on the sides before work
begins.

A newspaper is placed on the raised seat
For those who would rather read than stare at
the street.

III
For those who would rather read than stare at
the street
There's no shortage of things to read - posters
All over of sorcerers who can cure impotence,
make you meet
Your soulmate, double your money, align stars

Of fortunes in your favor - all kinds of things.
Workers are waiting for the foreman in small
Groups at a construction site, one of them
brings
Out their tools from a makeshift store near the
wall

As the rest try to ignore the early morning chill
With small talk. Little clouds of mists forming
around
Their mouths as they speak. A few minutes will
Be lost this way before someone hears the
sound

Of the vehicle when the foreman comes, clad in
a jacket
Like a farmer taking her produce to the market.

IV
Like a farmer taking her produce to the market
A mother is walking her 6-year-old son to
school.
Dressed heavily, and on his back a bag with a
packet
Of snacks and crayons, he looks like a
parachute diver in full

Gear going to take a leap, though with a lost
Expression on his face. His mother holds him
by one hand
While she talks coquettishly on the phone, most
Unlikely with the father of the boy or her
husband.

The lady at the eatery is arranging her utensils
As she gets ready for the day. She wipes
The tables and moves chairs around them, she
fills
Plastic jugs with water from one of the pipes

In the kitchen, replaces the lids, and puts each,
On each table in the eatery. There's a bottle of
bleach

V

On each table. In the eatery, there's a bottle of
bleach,
Or syrup, that has been recycled and made
Into a saltshaker. The morning is yet to reach
It's peak and the eatery is full already. Bread

And rice are rarely ordered by those who eat
here
Because they are considered too light. A
preacher in a suit
Is shouting a sermon on the street, you can hear
Him from two streets away. He has put

A cup in front of him but people seem
To have ignored both of them as they walk
Past in a hurry. Probably it had occurred to him
That if he preaches on the street, people will
just fork

Out their money and give it to him. It's a
dream,
He'll know it when reality finally hits him.

VI

He'll know it when reality finally hits him
Later in the day, that people have other needs.
At a maternity waiting lobby, a man jolts from
a scream
Behind the doors, another life, another mouth
that feeds

And demands more - his bundle of love.
From this moment, his life has changed,
From this moment, his child's needs come above
His own. That's the way society is arranged.

It's another day of young jobseekers knocking on doors,
Another day of frustrations and disappointment,
Another day of facing the stark reality - who knows
You? That's the merit in companies and government.

But they don't give up, the more they are rejected the more
They wake up every morning and knock on every door.

VII
They wake up every morning and knock on each door
In the rich part of the city for any domestic
Chore they can do at a fee. These old women know
Which home is peaceful and which one is dramatic.

As the day begins, every corner has an activity
Going on - a struggle, an enjoyment and a suffering,

A happiness and a sadness, arrogance and
humility,
All in equal measure. The joys of life are in it's
living.

In the end every isolated activity is a scene
That is connected to other scenes and
collectively
They sum up into a play - with some that win
And some that lose. One can persuasively

Make a case that it's not wrong to say
A day unfolds it's self like a play.

I tried

I tried so hard to keep it inside me
As you stretched out your arms
For a hug, or as you raised
Your palm up for a high-five.

I tried so hard to keep it inside me
As we sat at a table to eat
And you called me a 'good friend',
Patted me on the shoulder, as you laughed
With your mouth full of food.

I tried so hard to keep it inside me,
As you talked about how rich you were,
How you know who and who in government,
Yet you have not paid me for six months.

I try it so hard to keep it inside me,
When I have to go and fetch
Those silly girls of yours at ungodly hours,
While your wife is crying at home.

Let it be

For the wind that blows,
Let it blow,
For the wind will blow.

For the river that flows,
Let it flow,
For the river will flow.

For a tear that drops,
Let it drop,
For a tear will drop.

For a smile that crops,
Let it crop,
For a smile will crop.

For a love that is lost,
Let it be lost,
For a love will be lost.

For a heart that grows,
Let it grow,
For a heart will grow.

For the hair that greys,
Let it grey,
For the hair will grey.

For the sun that sets,
Let it set,
For the sun will set.

The Path

There is a path in my mind,
Cuts through the greenest grass
Tall just to my ankles,
Wide enough just for one.
Every night in my sleep
As I watch the sunset,
I stroll on it with a smile.
I know all its bends
And all its stones,
It has no mud or dust.
I suspect nobody else knows
About this path,
I have never met anybody else.
I have never known where
It leads to or comes from
Because I never reach its end,
I don't even know how
I find myself on it.

The lost wind

This must be a lost wind
Meant to blow somewhere else,
It must have lost its direction,
I can tell from the way it smells.

Winds that blow here smell a baby's breath,
They just tremble and never break reeds in
water,
I have seen them since childhood,
When I was my father's daughter.

This one must've hurried to get out and blow
And not waited for the right directions from
The god of winds. Look how it blows
With fury and energy of a storm.

The Altar

I've finally found a place to sneak
To when am tired and weary of what
The world just throws at me to break
My heart and tear my hopes apart.

A lucky stumble that must've been,
Discovering such a place of peace,
Amazing view I'd never seen
Before I felt unnerved on my knees.

The grass is green and soft on touch,
With silky blades and edges smooth,
And flowers glow - compete to catch
Your gaze among themselves with truth.

The silence laps on shores unseen,
I float on wings of moaning voice,
My closet secrets come out clean,
And nerves burn without a choice.

Who will carry me home?

Who will carry me home
When the moon drops down
And breaks its york
On my head?

Who will carry me home
When the hooded angel of death
Raises his dreaded scythe
And strikes at my heart?

Who will carry me home
When the breath of Satan
Gets into my lungs
And stops them?

Who will carry me home
When the sky thunders in lightening
Of rage and unknown revenge
And strikes me blind?

Who will carry me home
When the silent wind of ghosts
That blows without raising dust
Carries my soul away?

Back in the Days

We sang all the songs we could remember,
And repeated them all over again,
Someone blew a ram's horn
And another one played the tin drums,
We danced in the moonlight.

We opened our mouths to the sky and howled,
To let the spirit of childhood out of our chests,
We jumped and chased one another,
We wrestled and carried each other,
We played in the moonlight.

We rolled in grass and listened to crickets,
We laid on the threshing ground and counted
stars,
We sang to the moon until it smiled
Back to us and we giggled,
We laughed in the moonlight.

We enjoyed in the moonlight.

Wounds and Salt

Daughter of a woman, please take it slow,
The centre has become as hard as a rock,
The way you are doing it, I can't take it
anymore.

Why are you taking me to where beasts go?
You lead me along the path without talk,
Daughter of a woman, please take it slow.

You have just poked my virility at the core,
And my ship has already sailed off the dock,
The way you are doing it, I can't take it
anymore.

The pod has dried in the sun and will blow
And spill its seeds on the ground to crop,
Daughter of a woman, please take it slow.

My eyes are fixed at the closed door
Yet I cannot hear anyone knock,
The way you are doing it, I can't take it
anymore.

You are rubbing salt in wounds that are raw,
My fear-soaked legs are not able to walk,
Daughter of a woman, please take it slow,
The way you are doing it, I can't take it
anymore.

The Village old Lady

There lived a lady by the path,
Where children from villages passed
To school in the dawn
Then back at the gloam,
Enjoying the kicking of dust.

She lived alone and was old,
No child, or a cat, or a dog,
A soul did not go
To greet or to gab,
Her world was just her's in her hut.

The thieves did not steal her chicken,
And mothers with children would push
Their faces behind
Their skirts when she passed,
Avoiding the spell in her eyes.

She cooked her fish in the night
And threw the sharp bones at the path
To wound the children
And cause them anguish
At dawn, on their way to the school.

She watched from cracks in her wall
And burst in a hiss of a laugh,
To show her brown teeth,
And wiped the tears
Of joy, as they limped in pain.

An Aubade

The morning comes rewarding their sweet
cheer,
Much jubilation long before first ray,
They dare not sleep but wait another day
Of chanting tunes to all who care to hear.
And dusk will come to find them still that way
Excited, thought that day is coming near
To close won't break their hearts and bring a
tear,
And each will want her song in air to stay.

Their hearts will never know a pain any worst
Than sinking grain, their world has nothing sad,
They think no future life to come or past,
And won't recall a thing or insult heard,
They're free and live a life of joy that last,
It's why a time I wish I was a bird.

Me? A Witch?

If I were a witch
Would I have let you into this home?
If I were a witch, tell me young lady,
Would I have let him grow
Into a man you saw and fell for?

I welcomed you with open arms
And gave you the three stones
To start you by and make you comfortable.
I accommodated your silly eccentricities
That you said were modern ways.
Now you have urinated your last
In this homestead.

Let me tell you, young woman,
He is mine too, and he will always be.
I opened my legs for him
Wider than you ever will.
I bathed and kept him warm,
What makes you feel that
The sun rises and falls in your eyes?

You will leave,
You will take your bones back to your people,
And he will marry another woman,
A woman with a proper bottom.
I don't even want to see your painted face,
You look like a ghost.
You will leave.

Luthekhe

A final check on the straws, they should be
enough for all,
They are made from stems of a climbing plant,
Cut and left out for insects to eat away the pith
Before the straw maker blows the insects out
And puts a metal sieve at one end.

Everything has to be ready before tomorrow,
Because tomorrow is the day for *luthekhe*.
The seats have to be enough too,
The brew was set three days ago
And tomorrow it will be at the peak.

Tomorrow they'll start trickling in early,
The men of the village,
Some with their own straws, some without,
Some in groups, some solitary.
They'll come because I sent out word
That I will be brewing *luthekhe*.
One is never a man enough if he has never
brewed
And invited men of the village for the drink.

They will sit around a pot of the brew,
Each seeping from the pot
With their straws as they talk.
The woman of the home will keep
A steady supply of hot water.

Jokes will be cracked and
Youthful conquests recalled.
Disputes will be solved,
Friendships will be cemented
And monogamy laughed at.

No children will be allowed - or women,
They will drink and laugh
In praise of the host.

People

Some people go through life
Wearing only closed shoes,
As if they will face the knife
If they dared refuse.

Some think they will get far
In life if they smiled less
And looked focused and sober
Exclusively on their face.

After work, some still sacrifice
Their time in evening classes
Just so they get a pay raise,
And live differently from the masses.

Some search for a perfect husband
Or wife to marry, until they age,
That is when they understand
And turn to others in rage.

Some think they will eventually
Get rich and afterwards live happily,
By seeming busy and virtually
Being absent from their family.

Most in public stare in the eyes,
And open for each other the door,
Their mouths speak out lies,
Yet back home it's just a war.

I know some who borrow
Just so they remain at par
With friends or colleagues who follow
Trends and fashions that do not matter.

One day she woke up different

One day she woke up different,
Unencumbered, untethered and free.
She didn't plan it,
It just happened.
Maybe her back was finally on the wall,
Maybe the rope had reached its end,
Maybe she had reached her limit.
All she remembers the previous night;
The tears could not come out
After years of crying.
There was nothing more left to squeeze out.
Sleep from all the years had hit her
And devoured all her *mikosi* away,
That is how she woke up new.
She knew she will never cry again,
She was done with it.
Done with anything that didn't bring her
happiness,
Done with trying to figure out who was with
her,
Or against her,
Or indifferent because they didn't have the guts
to pick a side.
She realized that opinions are a-dime-a-dozen,
Validation was for parking,
And love, love? Love is not a word.
That life is too short to leave the key
To your happiness in someone else's pocket.

The Travel

It never requires you to come back home,
You just go until you can't go any more,
All you ever know is where you come from,
You will even be lucky to know what it is for.

Unexpected spells of pain never cease,
Crush your spirit and leave you hollow,
Sometimes, happy moments you later miss,
Each gives no sign what will follow.

You don't choose which road to take,
Go by whichever you find yourself on,
What matters are the tracks you make
And whether you leave good seeds sown.

Things change, but you change faster than you
want,
You keep walking on because you have no
choice,
Along the way are lessons you have learned,
Maybe someday, to a keen ear, you will voice.

The Man in the Mirror

The man that stands before myself
Is looking right at me because
We know another well enough.
We grew together keeping close,
I know the things that make him sad,
He knows the things I want so bad.

I try a smile and laugh a bit,
He weeps and smiles with pain at heart,
We look and see the sadness eat
Our souls and tear our hearts apart.
And though the mirror stands between,
We hold another shoulder-chin.

We look and see ourselves tied
In lies, we see our sadness stretch
From shore to shore, a seed that died
Within its shell. It's time to fetch
Some will and put a smile on man
Before me, begging fairness done.

Life

Wake and pick a flower of choice,
Smell and fill your lungs with its scent and
Let the feeling float you in air for
Seconds of pleasure.

Sit at the cliff and smile with the sinking sun,
Watch the world close its business for the day
As crickets and birds sing their farewells
In their best of voices.

Get lost in a forest that has no paths,
Lie on your back and let it tell you
Stories that were and stories that were not,
-and whispers of life.

Stand in the waterfall and spread your arms,
Let the water wash away the debris of the past.
Open your mouth and let the future
Pour into your heart.

Live a life of happiness and joy,
Seize what ought to be and let what is be,
Get the best out of each passing day,
Life is a blowing wind.

Rain

Come; Pour down in torrents and flood,
Gates of heaven, fling open, release
Your delicate small bags and I'll be glad.

Soak everything and fill the cracks please,
Turn all this soil flour into soft mud
That will slide through my toes with ease.

Come, Come, haven't you heard?
Through these valleys make water flow,
I'll make six boats to sail without guard.

Please come, for grass will grow,
I'll not have to see the next country,
Trees will grow and sway when winds blow.

Birds will sing to ease the sultry,
I'll climb up to find their nest
And place glue traps at their entry.

Then all these big birds will fly west
When all the meat in the field where
Cows were is over, it'll end their feast.

Perhaps Pa will stop staring in the air
And being quiet and perhaps Mo will
Stop crying - and stroking my hair.

Thoughts from a hut

Perhaps a thief should come and rob my hut
And find my rotting flesh and stench of death
That hangs around and never goes away.
Perhaps the playing boys should kick the ball
My way and come in looking left and right
To find my wasted body about to die.
Perhaps the dogs that comes at door and stare
At darkness inside barks and draws the ears
Of village men who sit beneath the tree.
Perhaps my roof of grass should catch a fire,
Then worried neighbours fight to put it out
So lest adjacent huts are also burnt,
To find my mirthless body here spread on mat.
Perhaps the roof should fall and smash my
body
For once and all, and save myself anguish.

The day the Monkey died

On that day, it's the silence that fell
In the forest that told of events
That happened. Things were not well,
On that day you could hear from the vents.
It was deafening whist.

And the birds were not chipping at all,
Like they do at that hour of the day.
It had scared the big and the small,
As if nature had stopped to pray.
It was silence of death.

On that day it's not known if the air
Was in motion. The sun was out though,
But the branches were still. It is rare
For the leaves not to swing with the flow.
It was hard to believe.

At a clearing. The monkey. It lay
On its back with her limps in a spread
And its intestines eaten away,
Much like eating the soft of the bread.
It was shocking indeed.

At the top was a patch where a flake
Of green lichens had peeled away
From the trunk. It had slipped from lack
Of a grip on a truck in its play.
So unfortunate. Sad.

A problem with lips

A girl is trying hard
To resist a smile that starts
To form on her face.

The more she resists
The more it pulls at the ends
Of her fuller lips.

Her lips are now tight,
A tooth starts to show,
Followed by another one.

Her lips part to smile
As her sweet eyes smile too,
A scene of beauty.

A laugh starts to build
In her chest,
She opens her mouth
To let it escape.

My little heaven

Many are there who wait for the day to get in
Heaven, let them wait and forever keep the
Rules lest Lord out locks them, I wish them
luck all.
They have their heaven.

But, my heaven rests her fair face asleep on
Folded arm and facing me, only one is and
Ever be. Her lips are a thing of magic.
All that I need is

Morning splash in coming from window 'cross
the
Room. And now she'll open those eyes and fire
will
Start in heart deep inside - I swear it - there,
ooh
Lord have a mercy.

Angels on a side street

Brushing me by the shoulders,
Rushing past on the side street,
Some with bags, some with folders,
Some staring, some discreet.
All with urgency on their face.
All walking at the same pace.

All walking on my street side,
Not even one on the other side across.
Why? They are taking each stride
With energy and without remorse.
Am I on a different land?
Something I don't understand?

'Why are you all going that way
And I am the only one going the other?
Where are you all headed to anyway?
Why is the other side empty further?'
She just briefly smiled at my eyes,
Then proceeded to walk on to paradise.

Unnerved

I should uproot the weeds and plant a row
Of beans. Perhaps some rain will fall and soak
The soil enough for them to grow and soar.
The silent night is dark, although alone
I should not close my sleepy eyes at all,
I cannot miss to see the sun at dawn.
I think I should just keep on kicking more,
And try with all my energy not to drown,
Perhaps the shore is near - you never know.
I have my mouth agape and facing up
The sky, perhaps a drop of water rich
In hope and faith will drop from heavens' tap.
I lack the strength to see another day,
The end is near and yet so far away.

Like a coin

The wind will sweep the feather up the roof
And swill around the air until it saps
To null and stillness, leaving air aloof,
Then down and slowly feather falls on laps.
The sun will shine to blind our eyes and burn
Our skins, but still the cold and darkness comes
Engulfing hills and seas, you'd think the sun
Will never come again to kill the worms.
A flower buds and snares the world with scent
And beautifulness, bright without a guilt,
Until it wakes and gets its vigour spent,
It fights but ultimately drools and wilt.
When life is blowing cold to you today,
Tomorrow life could blow a hot your way.

Contrition (An elegy to the fish)

They put hooks in your mouth,
After deceiving you with a piece of food.
With force they pull you forth
And take you, or return if you are not good.

They put your head on a hard place,
As they bring down a rod to smash.
They cut your belly and pull out the mess,
Which on the ground they splash.

They put you in boiling oil,
And devour your sides and eyes.
They don't bury your bones in the soil,
They leave them for the birds of the skies.

Sorry.

My heart now beats different

The wind blew away
The roof of my heart,
The rain socks the furniture
And the sun shines on weeds
Growing on my carpet.
My heart has become a ruin,
Thorns have overrun my heart,
Jackals haunt my kitchen,
Wild goats bleat at each other,
Night creatures sing in my heart.
Owls and ravens nest there,
Falcons gather, each with its mate.
My heart has become a garden,
A neglected ancient palace.
The weeds have killed contrition,
The smell of bat urine
Has chocked off sympathy.
The wolfs ate away the love,
The sun has scorched away humanity.

A message for the goose

Take my message to a far place,
Glide smooth on your light wing,
Flap and don't rest mid race,
I am sending you to go and sing.

Say that I apologize for all the wrong,
That I hold no ill feeling.
Mention that I have waited for long,
That it has been a long-time healing.

Look at me; I am a deprived shoot,
My sun has fallen west for the night.
Days go by but it has stayed put,
I stare east for a sign of light.

Things should not happen this way,
It's not fair; it's not fair at all.
It is a pity that I have to pay
And nobody wants to hear my call.

The boat ride

Stretch out your arms and row,
Don't talk of what we both know.
This sea has so many beasts,
The kind with horrifying visits.
They don't like to see our boat sail,
They'll do anything to see us fail.
Look ahead and brace for the ride,
We will reach the other side.
The angel that looks after doves
Will see to it that we have our nerves.

At the coffee shop

I saw beauty so rare,
Unfairly beautiful - a fairy's child,
Made my heart float on air.

Deep dark-sheened wild hair,
Slender fingers, nails well filed,
I saw beauty so rare.

Her smiley eyes were so fair,
She made my mind go wild,
Made my heart float on air.

God's finest jewel laid bare,
And so elegantly styled,
I saw beauty so rare.

Indifferent to itself, wouldn't care
Less, such demeanour so mild,
Made my heart float on air.

And as I watched the pair,
Wishes in my heart piled.
I saw beauty so rare,
Made my heart float on air.

The leopard must be giving birth

It's raining straight showers in the bright
Afternoon sun. Lucent drops compete each
Other to hit the ground as light
Murmurs fill the air from their touch.

A strong aroma of fresh earth
Fills my nostrils as its recurrent thirst
Get quenched. Soon, road and path
Will be too wet and slippery to walk fast.

An awkward stillness hangs right
Before my eyes, so solid I can catch.
Even birds are disturbingly quiet,
Perhaps they have also never seen such.

A leopard must be giving birth
Somewhere, at this exact moment at least,
So says the folklore, and the path
To the river is now a dance ground for the
beast.

I shall rise up again

I shall rise up again,
Stronger than I was before,
Am numb from any more pain.

I'll grow from this tiny grain
To the biggest tree the world ever saw,
I shall rise up again.

Though small as a drop of rain,
I will ripple to every shore,
Am numb from any more pain.

Never again will anyone drain
Energy from my spirit to the core,
I shall rise up again.

From today I will not entertain
Insouciance, I'll only knock on doors I know,
Am numb from any more pain.

Though painful, it has been good to train
My nerves, now I know I should not bow.
I shall rise up again,
Am numb from any more pain.

To a young one

I'll always pray for you each day and night
That stones and dust on path you follow turn
To gold, the road you take to turn out right.
Remember, fails and falls are times to learn.
Just speak the truth and watch the words you
say,
Your tongue is strong - a knife that cuts both
sides.
A careless word can turn a price to pay,
A clever word will sail above the tides.
When people smile at you don't bite that bait,
It's wise to look at deeds and watch if eyes
Indeed, do smile with lips. Avoid a trait
Before it turns around to give surprise.
My son, you need to know that men are born
To take a trip of faith in world unknown.

The discreet picker

If only you could talk,
Oh, the discreet picker,
If only we could hear you walk.

We'd tell you the funniest joke,
Quail you off with a big laughter,
If only you could talk.

We'd stay behind the lock
In silence until it is safer,
If only we could hear you walk.

Can't you even be polite and knock?
We'd give you the best excuse ever,
If only you could talk.

Even a tiny ant under the rock
Will not escape your hunger,
If only we could hear you walk.

So, do you live under the oak?
We'll send you a beautiful virgin sooner.
If only you could talk,
If only we could hear you walk.

Youth

I see them giggle and tease each other green,
Their faces bright, they smile with sparkling
eyes,
They ripple with joy and feel like birds in skies,
They walk and talk in manners never seen.
Without a doubt they hold the source of pride
Within their skins not knowing what it brings.
They want the world to know they're queens
and kings,
Any thought that cross their mind they want it
said.

Within no time the glow will fade away,
I pray and hope they get to learn some things,
Because mistakes they do will cost some day.
They ripe and glow then fall and rot like fruits,
The saddest part is when their seeds don't grow
To others. Youth is nothing absolute.

Captivity

I guess I should by now just go, instead
Of waiting here in vain. The chance of you
Appearing sink with sinking sun, the view
Isn't strong enough to make you leave my head.
I came in hope I'll get to see your face
Again, I thought you came here every day.
I need a heart to make me go away
And never feel the urge to watch this place.
A trail you went and left behind won't fade,
I wish I could just follow your sweet scent
That runs around my mind without an end,
It clouds my mind all day, from rise to bed.
For chance of luck and fate am captive held,
Isn't fair to punish me for things beheld.

A friend

When blowing winds of fear intend a lot
Of damage, blind your sight and want to blow
Away your stand, don't let your spirit bow,
Because I'll hold you close and give support.
When worlds' pursuits become so steep and
land
You, soaking wet in fright, in caves you dread,
As grip is slipping fast on that thin thread,
Don't sweat a thing, because I'll give a hand.
When roads and paths you trusted end in dark,
You look around your life for what it means
And close your eyes to think of all the sins.
Believe my word because I have your back.
I'll always stand with you and do you more,
Because my love is truth you'll ever know.

My farewell villanelle

This time I have to get up and go,
And I will not look back,
It doesn't matter anymore.

I have to walk through that door
Today before it is dark,
This time I have to get up and go.

I will be long gone before
You come whistling from 'work',
It doesn't matter anymore.

This time you have hit the core,
You have widely passed the mark,
This time I have to get up and go.

When the wound is still raw
I have strength to fill my sack,
It doesn't matter anymore.

I won't again think of the vow,
I wish you all the best and good luck,
This time I have to get up and go,
It doesn't matter anymore.

Returning home

Oh Mother, where is a spot of warmth?
A lasting fire, my fingers are numb,
I have come from the abysmal depth
Of pain, the memories swell the lump.

Oh Mother, where is a beam of light?
A sign another day will come
In this fear-soaked forest night,
I can barely even move an arm.

Oh Mother, show me the road to take,
This time around I don't want any pain.
I need a smirk of luck to make
A choice not leading to swamps again.

Oh Mother, will you tell me?
I want to hear you say
That the next one will stay, what befell
Me is not my fate, I'll smile one day.

The winner

I ran the race, I searched tracks in shades
Of time, where lights don't reach. At times I
hear
A whisper start a laugh of mock, the ear
Just lets it in but fast as flash it fades.
I dreamt in cold and glimpsed life in stars,
I saw myself up almost touching skies
And woke to find a dream. I open my eyes
And make a pact to never follow mass.

Now look, am seated high at lofty place
Of influence, planning how to run this town.
Am confident no soul will pull me down,
I got it all because I won the race.
And looking back at crowds I've put to rout,
I guard my comfort zone and watch them pout.

Hunters

I see four of them walk across
The fields in the morning dew,
Lean, with a slight stoop
And a hungry look.
Three are carrying two clubs
And a blade knife at the hip,
One carries a sisal sack,
Flung on the left shoulder to the back.
A park of eager dogs sniffs around,
Tongues dropping from their open mouths.
The hunters stop to inspect something,
A sniffing dog leads them to a bush.
They start beating on the bush,
One shouts and the dogs break into a chase
With hunters behind in pursuit.
It is a rabbit.

To the spider

I watch you
Doing what you do,
What you know best.
Assiduous,
Serious,
Stitching here,
Joining there,
Pulling,
A thread issuing from behind,
Making rounds,
Making boxes,
Not resting,
Not stopping to look.

You pin together an artist's piece,
A splendid web,
A trap.

And then wait at a corner.
A fly buzz by,
Then plunge in your sticky web.
Then you come out,
For a meal.
Very clever.

After Everything

Tonight I am coming home,
To the place where I belong,
Am coming to the place I feel warm.

I am running away from
The world that is wrong,
Tonight I am coming home.

I am done with the roam,
My ears want the old song,
I am coming to a place I feel warm.

I have been through a storm
And it has been quite long,
Tonight I am coming home.

I know I have lost form,
But believe me, I am still strong,
I am coming to a place I feel warm.

Can we go back to the norm?
I am bringing someone along.
Tonight I am coming home,
I am coming to a place I feel warm.

Fear

I give you love, you turn away in fear,
Your heart was hurt before my heart. The world
Is full of pain and hearts that shed a tear,
Our chests are carrying hearts that freeze in
cold.
But why don't you just close the door from past
And stop reliving moments gone away.
At times, some things are never meant to last
For long, don't let the past to spoil your day.
So, come, I want to show you ways to trust
Again, I watch you smile and see behind
The smile, the fear of pain. You want to cast
The line but scared stiff of what you'll find.
You see, am just like you - afraid to dare.
We are a perfect pair - afraid to care.

Love

I believe in love.
I believe in the completeness
One finds in another.
And I believe in the helplessness
Of teenagers in love.
I believe in the idea that love is a choice,
And the understanding of a matured love;
Knowing without them speaking.

I believe in the comfort of presence,
The silence that goes unnoticed,
The goofy intimacy of brushing teeth together,
Talking over the day's events
In an unintelligible foamy garble.
I believe in the uninhibited milieu of lovers
Pouring out their hearts to each other,
Sharing their life's intimate details
And finding comfort in vulnerability and trust.

I believe in love,
The pain it brings,
The agony of grief
And in the shared pain between lovers.

I believe in love
And absence of love,
Or lack of reciprocity.
I believe in the ending of love too.

A childhood game

When I pass past those bushes
And see their ruffled branches,
An empty tin with a little ball nearby,
I know some boys have tried to tie
Them close together.

 They have been playing that game,
The game of calling out enemies by name
And revealing their hiding place
As they come out showing their face
In defeat.

They use the tin to cover the ball
Then hide to wait for the call.
Meanwhile, trying not to be seen
They run to go and kick the tin
To win the game.

The supervisor

At the factory where I work,
The supervisor has a stern stare,
Looking down at us stooped
Over our work at our posts.

Passes through the factory each day,
Enters by the door on one side
And leaves by the one on the opposite,
How he passes - passes without speaking.

His face is beautiful when he enters,
He stares harshest when he is midway
But nice to look at when he leaves.
The East and West know his beauty.

A girl

There was a girl - a lovely girl,
Who lost her love through her indifference,
A soul that cared - that went unshared,
Until it died within her silence.

Tightly holding onto her heart,
Too afraid to give and lose again,
Such a solid wall she had built
Against the most boisterous storm rain.

The eyes could not smile with her face
Even to a benign coquettish being.
A heart that goes unshared,
I've heard it said, dies yearning.

Tired

I walk around my mind in this long night,
Just when am hoping dawn will come very
soon
Its dusk of yet another night of fright,
I face another night without a moon.
I crawl in scorching sun and search a drop
Of water, thirsty, losing strength so fast.
In front, the sight of oasis gives me hope,
I walk to drink but find a bowl of dust.
Am falling fast in space unknown, my being
Is numb from fright. My starving body has
grown
To lifeless stones, my fingers feel a thing
And clasp so tight but learn it's just a gown.
At times I think about my future life
And want to slit my wrists with sharp a knife.

Prayer of a sick man

I want to say this quickly lest you think
That I gossip around about you
And turn your hungry teeth on me.
Let me make my plight
In a blink of a time.
I ask you for a favour,
When you come for me,
Come when everyone else is asleep.
I don't want to see them weep
As they watch me go.
Please,
Come during the harvest season,
When granaries are full of food,
Friends and family should not
Mourn me on empty stomach.

Childhood remembered

I remember waking up early
And sneaking to the fields,
To make patterns in the dew,
In the bright rising sun.
Walking, kicking and splashing
The lucent drops off the soft grasses,
Tall just above my ankles,
As I made my way through.
Making patterns I desired
With my greener trails.
Then with sterile clean toes
Returning home with a smile.

I remember the murmurs
Of maize plantations,
Turgid stems and broad leaves
At their greenest and waxiest,
Trembling to the slow breeze
In the mid-morning sun.
Plucking the fine mane
From their developing pistils
And spreading on my forehead,
My head tilted to the sky.
Smiling at a group of birds
Gliding smoothly in circles,
Their wings spread out wide,
- enjoying too.
I remember the rollercoaster rides
On top of a banana trunk,
On slopes of the anthills.
Occasionally slipping off the trunk
And riding on my bare bottom.

I remember returning home
To find wild chicken,
Stuffed with rice
And cooked over wood fire,
So delicate it makes you cry.

Am blessed

Some people cannot jump to grasp
Branches hanging high above the path.
Some cannot reach out to step on the dry leaf
That looks crunchy on the side walk.

Some will never know the beauty
Of a sunset, the serenity of the sea,
Or even the sadness of a waterfall,
No matter how explicitly they are told.

Some will never be soothed by music,
To them, the singing bird in the distance
Does not exist, just as the crickets.
Silence sounds no worse than a baby' giggle.

Sit up

Just sit up and wipe that tear,
It's about time to face the crowd,
Things will soon be fine my dear.

This is the moment to conquer the fear,
A time to try again and smile loud,
Just sit up and wipe that tear.

Stand up and hold your heart near,
We all have at one time sat on a cloud,
Things will soon be fine my dear.

The past is already gone, like last year,
A single fault should not leave you bowed,
Just sit up and wipe that tear.

Turn a deaf ear to whatever you hear,
Look ahead and remember what you vowed,
Things will soon be fine my dear.

I know right now things are not clear,
But when all is through, you'll be proud,
Just sit up and wipe that tear,
Things will soon be fine my dear.

The servant

Today I have attended to my place of work,
The place assigned to me in this castle,
My responsibility is around my neck like a
yoke.

I made a pact with myself that little by little
I will eventually get my section of the wall
clean,
As much as possible I will keep off the wits
battle.

Each day I will wake up and go back at it, keen
And humbly work it until it is sparkling bright.
Even if it kills me, this will be my big win.

Meanwhile, I do not mind what others might
Be doing or whether they are asleep,
It's not my worry if they are wrong or right.

I will not let any circumstance that comes keep
Me from my work. Nobody will break my
heart,
Because the seeds of my strength are planted
deep.

When the day comes, I will have played my
part,
I will look at my bright section and smile,
If the whole castle will not be bright I will not
hurt.

The Dirt

Bring the wind to wash away
Demons back to the sea.
Scoop them from my palm
And take them to the distant horizon
Away from my conscience.

Let it rain all day
And wash away the dirt
From my childhood.
Let it even flood,
I can't shed enough tears,
I want all the water,
I want a river,
I want a sea,
To swim through
And come out the other side,
Or the other me.

But don't bring the sun
To wilt the demons,
To dry the demons,
And leave scars.

The standing Tree

In grazing field there is a standing tree,
Alone in open field where grass is dark,
Imposing heed to all with scaly bark,
Its massive size the blind at once agree.
No soul has seen it grow or branches shoot,
At times a few old leaves may drop to ground
And dry, when walking, make a crunchy sound,
The inner branches won't be seen at root.
In strongest winds it never bends a bit,
The leaves just tremble and give a scaring roar,
And whether the sun does burn or rain does
pour
It stands unchanged, counting decades fleet.
We came and found it here the way it is
And green it'll be the time our days do cease.

Loneliness

The hut is standing bold in this bright night,
Its muddy walls that give shy beams of light
From holes in them reflect their strife to cope,
Dry grass that thatches roof completes its
shape.
Inside the closed door a steady flame
Is standing on the tip of a tin lamp, calm,
Its cones at rest upon another in frail,
With brighter outer issuing sooty tail.
A wrinkled face looks at flame very keen,
The palm with knobbed fingers carries chin,
The mind is far and questions flood its soul,
Hard questions that have no answers at all.
This life with gifts that it gives to us isn't fair,
For those without their own, no one else cares.

Waiting for work

We queue before the gates of heavy metal,
Each quiet, it seems nobody knows another,
Each minding his business, like cudding cattle,
Nothing odd about complete strangers standing
together.

The lucky few will be taken to work for the day
When the gates open this morning – unloading
bags
Of cereals from container trucks. Then the pay
Later that evening.

A neighbour's description is all experience I
have.
I glance at my mates; broad shoulders, ashy
knuckles,
Jaundice eyes, and they seem to be chewing on
something.
So unlike me, with soft hands from years in
lecture halls.

Shock

My whole body is numb
And my mind is blank from what
My eyes have just seen.

I try to move my
Fear-soaked limps as I crawl
On the floor, naked.

My shivering body
Is covered in sweat and I
Cannot hold back the tears.

Oh, I should never
Have looked in that mirror
On my bedroom wall.

Will someone please close the gate?

It is quickly getting dark and late,
I cannot say it has got me by surprise,
Will someone please close the gate?

That was the most beautiful sunset,
 What we are left with are changing skies,
It is quickly getting dark and late.

It has been a good day by any rate,
Anything that starts eventually dies,
Will someone please close the gate?

Seeing the sun succumb to its recurrent fate
Is always a fresh breath to my eyes,
It is quickly getting dark and late.

I will give them food and get everything set
Because they will be gone again before sunrise,
Will someone please close the gate?

Though I have not seen a flower moment yet
I know I have to maintain the ties.
It is quickly getting dark and late,
Will someone please close the gate?

They took him to war

Somewhere under the stars
A girl sings,
Her sweet song floats
Over the huts.
A song with words
From deep in her heart.
Her voice has a scent
That longing brings.
Her's is the only loneliness,
Her heart yearns
For heaven that was.
She will never know
What happiness is
Until the source comes back,
And comes back alive.
They took him to the war,
That tallness sold him off.

Questions

So, how have you benefited
From breaking my heart?
What gains have you reaped?
What fortune have you struck?
Tell me.

What good has it done to you
To see me hurt this much?
Show me the bright side of it
That am too blind to see?
Talk.

What better person have you become
By putting me through anguish?
What sort of relief have you got
From putting my heart through hell?
Speak.

What am I paying back for?
Which kind of humour do you get
When you see me dying inside?
Why do you have to punish me?
Say it.

The planter

With that thin hoe she plants the rows
Of seeds, some short, some shorter, still
She aims and casts her seeds with laws
Of nature pressing down her will.

She digs in richer darker soil
Without a song or hum to cheer
Her spirits, days and nights of toil
Will make her sleep without any fear.

She rests awhile and looks at skies
To check the clouds for signs of rain,
A distant cloud has caught her eyes,
She knows it'll rain to ease the pain.

Life

Of all unending schooling, toiling, strife,
And high attention seeking just to get
The top position. Targets met and life
All spent on work, the schedules kept to date.
Forever chasing bigger cheques and car,
A bigger house, a cooler trend will come
And go, a style of life to get us far
Above the rest without inflicting harm.

Perhaps the money, wealth and houses lie,
They hold your gaze and fill your dreams with
junk.
Along the way in chasing things you die
And leave your family sad and rich with hate
Because you left them long before you died.
It's wise to live the life before it's late.

A schoolboy note

I do not know about your heart but mine,
I have love for you that never dies,
All I need from you is just a sign.

I dread the idea that you may decline,
Then throw me into that crowd that lies,
I do not know about your heart but mine.

I will take you to that distant line
Where the land meets the skies,
All I need from you is just a sign.

I could not comprehend being in cloud nine
Before I gazed into your sweet eyes,
I do not know about your heart but mine.

On the days I don't see you, I am never fine,
For you, there's nothing I can't sacrifice,
All I need from you is just a sign.

If it was something I could define
I would have shouted it from the rooftop at
sunrise,
I do not know about your heart but mine,
All I need from you is just a sign.

The drop of water

It gathers slower than it should,
Takes its own time to swell,
Forever growing to maturity,
At its own pleasure.
Testing my thirst and nerves,
Testing my patience.
Then it holds steady,
To decide.
We stare at each other,
For long.
My jaw gets tied,
I close my mouth for a moment,
To swallow my spit.
It then drops, on my chin.

Four Stanzas

She laughs it off and brushes it away
With a wave of hand in talks with her friends,
A girl deserves better, say
Her friends who know various trends.

She laughs with her lips and cries in her eyes,
Her heart encloses anguishing pain
From broken pleas of love and lies,
Afraid to try and lose again.

She wonders why it doesn't wait,
Another chance is gone in smoke,
All through she thought that that was it,
And now in pain she wishes he spoke.

A thought flashes across her mind,
To ask and trust the one above.
She wants to put the past behind
And wait another chance of love.

Come out

Come out and meet me my love,
Come and walk with me in the staring moon,
Let us cast a spell on the stars above.

I want to feel every curve
Of your frame - as smooth as a spoon,
Come out and meet me my love.

Step out and see what you have
Under the moon at its noon,
Let us cast a spell on the stars above.

Lapping waves are breaking on my nerve,
Slightly shifting the abandoned harpoon,
Come out and meet me my love.

Come out and feel what I have to serve,
Don't think I am leaving any time soon,
Let us cast a spell on the stars above.

I adore you so much my dove,
Come out of your glass cocoon,
Come out and meet me my love,
Let us cast a spell on the stars above.

The road

It never ends, just stretches out
And wide to farther places known
To men who lost their minds in war.
Sometimes it turns to right or left
But still it stretches on and on.
It takes the men away to where
The river takes it's dirt without
Returning home. They walk with ease
Like floating leaves that go to where
The currents takes them at will.
The wise have known this road for long
And seen it take the men away
For years without a try themselves.

The awakening

I lay alone in bed recalling days
That went when love (the feigned kind) was
rife
And rains of praises came in torrents. Raise
Your lash, Oh Lord of just, and whip my wife.
What happened? Gone, the radiant smile that
stood
On lips, coquettish laugh and humble way
She treated me when I was able and good,
The times I brought her monthly bread on tray.
So, now she comes at home before the dawn
In pomp and tut; 'from bars to look for food
For you and kids'. My home and heart are torn
Apart and anger burns like fire on wood.
The truth now sifts on me like ash in face,
Now every piece begins to fall in place.

Another year gone

Another year gone to the past,
I am glad it was not my last.
I thank my creator for life
And pray that I continue to thrive.
I thought it'll turn to the worst
As it has happened in the past.
A lot of people have died along,
Others have been found on the wrong,
But your love has kept me near,
To see yet another year.
One day I will sing you a song
Of praise and honour all day long.

The solitary bird

Behold the solitary bird,
Perched on the inside branches
High above the red path,
Where the grasses are soft.
Burying its head in its armpits,
Searching for things unknown.
Ruffling its feathers,
Straightening its quills
With its beak.
Stopping for a moment
To look in all directions
Then back at it again.

The week ahead

Sunday shuts down on this sunny evening,
Stocks, politics, sports - a neighbour's radio
sing,
A single wooden window and a makeshift bed
Define the small room. The boy, his head
In the cups of his hands, lies on his back.

He's listening to the periodic bang of a hammer
On metal from the workshop around the corner.
The bang always comes on his second
inhalation,
He coughs and shifts lightly, impressed by that
fortuity,
His mind then shifts to the week ahead.

He thinks of the words he has been hearing
For the past five years, now they ring
In his mind; 'currently we're fine, but if a
vacancy
Arises we'll get in touch with you in urgency.'
Such a lie - a verbal placebo.

He rises, stretches, and wipes his face,
Erasing the failures of years like a haze.
He sees his decent dark suit laid out,
His fare on the shelf beside the newspaper cut-
out,
And degree papers - first class honours.

In the sea

The boisterous winds are blowing hard,
The waves are eager to swallow me
Between their rising lips. A bad
And dangerous storm is coming, I can see
It fast approaching, heavy green
Clouds hanging low are closing in.

My heart is beating fast and sharp,
My hands are stiff from the hard grip
On bulwark. Feet are soaked damp
With fear, too rigid to even trip.
My lips just ripple in fray,
A tremble, a weak effort to pray.

A few minutes later, the sea is back
To normal, tranquil view extends
To ends of the world as gulls embark
On their smooth glides. The sky sends
My mind to dreams. Occasional frights
Is what my time in the sea consists.

My song

Give me back my song,
You took my song away
And did my heart wrong,
You blackened my heart's day.

The song I treasured most,
The one I sang from my heart
Is now forever gone and lost,
The one thing I'd lose last.

How will I step in the light
Without my song? I want to move
Out of the shadows' fright,
Away from this falling roof.

He plays games with his kids

He plays games with his kids,
The timely arriving and departing father,
They've never discovered his tricky deeds.

He departs from them slowly and bids
Them goodbye, never again to see each other,
He plays games with his kids.

Leaves them singing the elegy and creeds
For him while he is gone further,
They've never discovered his tricky deeds.

He then steals to the opposite door and
proceeds
To enter with all the gaudy he can gather,
He plays games with his kids.

Surprised, all his kids awake and leads
The world to sing in jubilation to one another,
They've never discovered his tricky deeds.

Sometimes he hangs aprons or beads
Over his kids to change the weather.
He plays games with his kids,
They've never discovered his tricky deeds.

Worries

I worry that the rains will soon stop
And the earth will swallow the last drop
And still be thirsty,
Then get annoyed
And shave off all its hairs
And leave the graves bare.

I worry that the trees will get sick
And stop dropping mangoes,
Then the leaves will turn yellow
And start falling off
To leave dry sticks pointing to the sky,
Like nails on the fingers of the devil.

I worry that the sun will soon set,
And darkness will rush to fill up
Any spaces that it finds,
Like an evil smoke,
Then roll my eyes backwards
And make them shed tears
From what they see inwards.

Letter to the wind

Carry me away with you,
Let me hang on your tails,
Because my day is well overdue
And my patience now fails.
I can't wait any longer.

Right where the sky kisses the sea
Is where I now long to go,
Far away from this hypocrisy,
I am no longer a local.
I am done.

I came, I saw and did not conquer,
Truth has now dropped on my face
Like an egg yolk, I have no hunger.
No man can ever win this race.
Now I know.

I don't see the need for another day,
Some things have nothing to do with age,
Please come and take me away,
I do not even have any luggage.
I am waiting.

Face of Ages

The world moved on and left
Me behind, lying in the field
Looking up in the sky. Bereft
Of energy to move and shield

My face from the scorching sun
And the unforgiving rain.
I've learnt to let the sun burn
As I hold in the pain

As well as hold my breath in the rain.
Now I watch the sky day after day,
Night after night, year and again.
I've seen the night sky in grey

And in pitch black, the stars
Have paraded their best for me.
I've seen all kinds of clouds pass,
The grey, the smoky ones and the foamy,

As well as the thunderstorms and the rainbow.
One time a lightning struck away
My eyelashes they had to all grow
Back afresh. Each day

Is different, occasionally, migrating
Birds fly by in formation,
Or a wild animal comes sniffing
And walk away in any direction.

A parakeet

I look at you and think how lucky one
I am to have a pretty thing like you,
And how I can't replace you with a new,
Or even live with absence of my sun.
I know you can't hurt me bad enough
To make me give it up and walk away,
To pine away alone. I'll stay each day
And be with you in waters calm or rough.
I keep the secret close, you'll never know,
A hot and cold I will still blow
To keep you guessing around
The clock. Careful though, lest a heart is
wound.
When all is said and done, this life
Is about keeping what is best to oneself.

The war field

I have set my eyes on the target,
I will ignore the flies crossing my view,
Waiting alert and fully set
For the opportune time to take my cue.

I have no time for side shows,
I will lose the battles but win the war.
This is a creed only my heart knows,
The secret energy keeping me on the go.

When I unexpectedly finally pounce
I will hit with every fibre of my being
Where it hurts most. Because this chance
Could be the only one there is in the offing.

For all there is to this short life,
I will take the best it has to offer
And not relent in this stiff strife
Or worry my heart when things differ.

In pain, I have finally come to know
That it is a war, a fierce silent war,
Where victory opens paradises' door
And defeat lands you on a rough shore.

Sunset

I came to the top of the rock,
High above the big oak
And looked west for the horizon,
And right there I saw
A splendid silent sunset.
So polite, so tender, so beautiful,
A few inches shy of touching the horizon.
There was nobody else in the world
But just the two of us.
I was looking at a pretty girl,
Smiling at me looking at her.

A day

Another day has come to a close,
Gone like a whiff of smoke,
Amazing how a thing just goes
Never to return even in a mock.

Tomorrow there'll come another,
But nothing like has ever been.
It may have the same weather,
But a cloud spread you have never seen.

You may go to the same places
And do things exactly the same way
You did last time, but not the same faces
Will say the same words the entire day.

You may even take the same road
At the same time and pace you did,
But not the same birds on tree with broad
Leaves will be jumping on branches to feed.

That's why I sometimes just smile
When I think of another day to come,
With surprises it hides for a while,
I look forward to it, it's bringing me some.

Easter Sunday Chant

Rejoice my heart for He is risen,
Climb on the hill and blow the horn,
All the chains of captivity are now broken.

The sins of our fathers are all forgiven
And the curses in our shadows are all gone,
Rejoice my heart for He is risen.

He is now seated on the chair that is golden,
Seated high with His father at the throne.
All the chains of captivity are now broken.

On the wall of heaven victory is written,
The curtains of darkness have been torn,
Rejoice my heart for He is risen.

He has taken away the sins of all men,
All the wars of men have been won,
All the chains of captivity are now broken.

All the kings of the world have fallen
And at the seat of power He sits alone.
Rejoice my heart for he is risen.
All the chains of captivity are now broken.

Farewell to the love
We gave to others
Like we didn't need it ourselves
And never got it back.

END

About the Author

S. Haya is a poet whose writing is informed by the interesting intricacies of human life.

Twitter @SHayawrites

hayasofficial@gmail.com